I0807052

My First Animal Library

Black Bears

by Jenna Lee Gleisner

Bullfrog Books

Ideas for Parents and Teachers

Bullfrog Books let children practice reading informational text at the earliest reading levels. Repetition, familiar words, and photo labels support early readers.

Before Reading

- Discuss the cover photo. What does it tell them?
- Look at the picture glossary together. Read and discuss the words.

Read the Book

- "Walk" through the book and look at the photos. Let the child ask questions. Point out the photo labels.
- Read the book to the child, or have him or her read independently.

After Reading

- Prompt the child to think more. Ask: Have you ever seen a black bear? Where was it, and what was it doing?

Bullfrog Books are published by Jump!
5357 Penn Avenue South
Minneapolis, MN 55419
www.jumplibrary.com

Copyright © 2019 Jump! International copyright reserved in all countries. No part of this book may be reproduced in any form without written permission from the publisher.

Library of Congress Cataloging-in-Publication Data is available at www.loc.gov or upon request from the publisher.

ISBN: 978-1-62496-756-6 (hardcover)
ISBN: 978-1-62496-757-3 (ebook)

Editor: Kristine Spanier
Book Designer: Leah Sanders

Photo Credits: Lynn_Bystrom/iStock, cover, 12; Stephen J. Krasemann/Getty, 1; Josef Pittner/Shutterstock, 3; Mark Raycroft/Minden Pictures/SuperStock, 4; Dean_Fikar/iStock, 5; FRANKHILDEBRAND/iStock, 6–7; Mikael Males/Dreamstime, 8; Ian Mcallister/Getty, 9; Daniel Friend/iStock, 10–11; nickjamesstock/iStock, 13; BGSmith/Shutterstock, 14–15; Chris Erasmus/Shutterstock, 15, 23br; critterbiz/Shutterstock, 16–17, 23tr; Wayne Lynch/Getty, 18–19, 23ml, 23bl; RGB Ventures/SuperStock/Alamy, 20–21, 23tl; Meagan Jenkins/EyeEm/Getty, 22; Ad_hominem/Shutterstock, 23mr; KenCanning/iStock, 24.

Printed in the United States of America at Corporate Graphics in North Mankato, Minnesota.

Table of Contents

Sniffing for Food

A black bear stands on its back legs.

Sniff. Sniff.

What does it smell?

Food!

Black bears have a great sense of smell.

They find fruit.

What else?
Honey. Bugs.

They catch fish, too!
Black bears eat a lot.

Most black bears live in forests.

They are the smallest bears in North America.

Short claws help them climb trees.

Why?

To get food.

Or sleep.

And to get away from predators.

Grizzly bears chase them!

The fur is thick.
It keeps them warm.
Most of them are black.
The muzzle is lighter.

muzzle

Black bears hibernate in winter.

Where? In dens.

Mothers have cubs in the den.

They come out in spring.

Time to eat!

Parts of a Black Bear

Picture Glossary

cubs
Baby bears.

muzzle
An animal's nose and mouth.

dens
Caves or holes where bears make homes during winter.

North America
The continent that includes the United States, Canada, Mexico, and Central America.

hibernate
To spend the winter sleeping or resting.

predators
Animals that hunt other animals for food.

Index

To Learn More

Learning more is as easy as 1, 2, 3.

1) Go to www.factsurfer.com

2) Enter "blackbears" into the search box.

3) Click the "Surf" button to see a list of websites.

With factsurfer.com, finding more information is just a click away.